Pieces Of Me

Every word is a wound, every page is a scar

Ceasar D'costa

Made with ❤ on the BookLeaf Publishing Platform
www.bookleafpub.in
www.bookleafpub.com

Dedication

To the moments that shaped me—the quiet ones that whispered wisdom, the stormy ones that tested my strength, and the fleeting ones that became memories I carry like sacred verses.

To the love that shattered me, breaking me open in ways I never imagined, teaching me the weight of longing, the ache of absence, and the beauty of having felt something so profound.

To the words that found me in the wreckage, that gathered my scattered pieces and stitched me back together—not as I was before, but as someone stronger, someone softer, someone who now understands the language of both loss and love.

And to the one who remains a part of my soul—woven into my every breath, my every silence, my every unwritten and written word. No distance, no time, no absence can erase what was once felt so deeply. Some bonds defy the laws of the world; some connections exist beyond the limits of touch and presence.

This book is for you. Always.

Preface

Some stories are not just written; they are lived, felt, and carried within the soul long before they find their way onto paper. This book is one of those stories—a collection of emotions, moments, and memories that shaped me, broke me, and, in many ways, rebuilt me.

It is not just about love or loss, but about the spaces in between—the silence that speaks louder than words, the ache that lingers even after the pain has faded, and the unspoken truths that live in the heart long after they are left unsaid.

I write not just for myself, but for anyone who has ever loved so deeply that it changed them, for those who have known the kind of silence that echoes, and for those who believe in the power of words to heal even the deepest wounds.

This book is my offering to the ones who left, the ones who stayed, and the ones who will always remain—no matter the distance, no matter the silence.

With every page, may you find a piece of yourself within these words, and may they remind you that even in

heartbreak, there is beauty, and even in loss, there is love
that never truly fades.

With all my heart,
Ceasar D'costa

Acknowledgements

No book is ever truly written alone. It is woven from the love, support, and presence of those who stand by us—whether in words, in silence, or in the quiet spaces between.

To those who have been my strength, my guiding light, and my reason to keep writing—thank you.

To the one who inspired these words, who became both my greatest joy and my deepest ache—this book carries traces of you in every page. Even in absence, you have remained a part of me, shaping the very essence of my words.

To my family and friends, who have stood beside me in moments of doubt and darkness, lifting me with their unwavering belief—your love has been my refuge, and I am forever grateful.

To the readers who find pieces of themselves in these pages—this book is as much yours as it is mine. May these words bring you comfort, understanding, and the realization that you are never alone in what you feel.

And to the universe, to fate, to whatever unseen force has guided me through love, loss, and healing—thank you for giving me the gift of words to make sense of it all.

With all my heart,
Ceasar D'costa

A Melody of Us

I met a girl I never saw,
only a voice drifting through the air,
a melody woven in fate's quiet hands,
a sound so pure, it pulled me near.

No faces, no glances exchanged,
just words dancing in the silence.
Among a crowd of fifty souls,
only we felt the thread between us tighten.

She found me, or maybe I found her.
We spoke, and in that fleeting moment,
the world around us blurred to nothing,
and all that remained was the space we filled.

Time was cruel in its brevity—
the shortest love, the deepest bond.
We never touched, never met,
only voices, only echoes, only longing.

But love does not always need hands to hold,
nor eyes to recognize its face.
It lives in laughter, in midnight whispers,
in unsaid words that beat within the heart.

Yet love, no matter how strong,
bows before the weight of fate.
Our families drew the line,
and we stepped away, though unwilling.

Now, a year has passed in silence,
a year without her voice in my ears.
But if love is true, it never leaves—
it only waits, it only lingers.

First love may not always be the last,
but true love carves its mark forever.
And if she was my true love,
then she will always be the end of my story.

A Sculptor Without Clay

Though I am not a sculptor,
I could carve you from memory alone,
Every curve, every inch, every tiny detail,
Etched into the fabric of my mind.

It's true—we never met.
It's true—my hands never traced your skin,
Never felt the warmth of your breath,
Never held you close in the quiet of the night.

And yet, I have seen you more now
Than I ever did when you were mine.
You do not stand before me,
Yet I spend my days lost in your presence.

Your pictures, frozen in time,
Are the mirrors I live through,
A past I cannot touch,
But one I refuse to let fade.

I study them like sacred scriptures,
Each glance another prayer to what once was.
I have memorized the way your lips curve
Before laughter breaks free from them.

I know the way your fingers brush back your hair,
The way your eyes hold stories within them,
The way the light used to dance upon your skin—
Soft, golden, unshaken by time.

And so, in my solitude, I recreate you.
Not in marble, not in clay,
But in the quiet corners of my heart,
Where you have always belonged.

I run my fingers over your image,
Imagining the way they would feel against your skin.
Every inch of you, measured and memorized,
Every line of you, engraved into my soul.

You may be a dream I can never hold,
A love written in invisible ink,
But even dreams deserve to be lived,
Even ghosts deserve to be loved.

So I will sculpt you in my mind,
With hands that will never touch,

With eyes that will never tire,
With a heart that will never forget.

5

For love is not bound by presence,
Nor lost to the hands of time.
You are here, even when you are not,
And that is all that matters to me.

Yours, Without a Name

I speak of pain, and I speak of love—
words that can make you smile,
words that can make you cry,
words that hold the weight of everything
I have ever felt for you.

But tell me, does it really matter
if I am in a relationship or not?
Because love was never just a label,
never just a name written in promises
or a bond sealed by time.
It was never about possession,
about claiming, about belonging.

Love is more than two hands intertwined,
more than stolen kisses in moonlit silence,
more than whispered "I love you's"
that fade into the night.
Love is two souls colliding,
two energies finding a home

within each other's chaos.
It is the comfort in knowing
that someone, somewhere,
holds a piece of you within them,
even if the world separates you.

I don't need you to be mine forever
to love you.
I don't need you to say my name
with longing in your voice
for my heart to keep beating for you.
I can love you from a distance,
in silence, in shadows,
without ever needing to claim you.

I can love the memories of you,
the way your laughter still lingers
like a melody in my mind,
the way your words still hold me
even when you are nowhere near.
I can love the fragments of you
that life allowed me to keep,
the moments we shared,
the dreams we built
but never lived.

Yes, I am lost.

Yes, I am broken.
But I am in a relationship—
with your thoughts,
with the way you once looked at me,
with the echoes of the promises we made,
with the love we never spoke aloud
but always felt.

And even if you never hear it,
even if you never see it,
even if time erases me from your world—
I will still love you.
In the quiet of every night,
in the spaces where you once stood,
in the depth of my soul where you still exist.

And I always will.

Unforgiven Love

Memories never fade, they chase me still,
Through silent nights and whispers chill.
No matter how far, how fast I flee,
They find a way to anchor me.

It took me years to stand again,
To breathe beyond the ghost of pain.
Yet one small spark, one fleeting glance,
Revives the wounds, renews the dance.

I lost myself in love too deep,
Gave all I had—my soul to keep.
My pride, my strength, my self-respect,
I traded all for her neglect.

She knew my heart, its every beat,
And crushed it cold beneath her feet.
With sharpened words, with quiet spite,
She turned my day into endless night.

She pulled me up, then let me fall,
A deeper void, no light at all.
And still, I fought to mend the past,
To make a love that couldn't last.

But love without respect is pain,
A hollow vow, a binding chain.
Some love stories are not to be,
Not all are meant for history.

So here I stand, no more confined,
By love that left me lost and blind.
For some goodbyes are blessings too,
And love should never be a wound.

A Wish Beyond Life

Many have wishes, dreams to chase,
lists of things to do before the end.
I, too, have dreams—
but in every one of them, there is you.

While others dream of distant lands,
of skies they wish to touch,
my only wish is simple—
to find my way to you,
in this life or the next.

But if fate is cruel,
if life refuses to let our souls entwine,
then let me tell you the wish
that rests at the top of my afterlife's list.

When my heart stops beating,
when my skin turns pale,
do not let my heart be buried
beneath the weight of a world

that never let it reach you.

Rip it from my chest,
hold it in your hands,
and carve your name deep into its flesh,
where it has always belonged.

Then bury it, not in the cold silence
of an unmarked grave,
but near the place you live,
where the wind still carries your scent,
where the earth still knows your footsteps.

For in this life,
my heart has yearned for nothing but you.
If I could not hold you in life,
let me rest near you in death.
Let my heart find peace,
knowing that, even when I am gone,
a piece of me will always be home—
with you.

Because my heart was never mine to keep.
It belonged to you then,
it belongs to you now,
and it will belong to you
Always & Forever.

Maybe, Just Maybe

I have always tried to reach you,
in ways words could never capture,
in the silence between my breaths,
in the spaces where my heart still whispers your name.

I have always tried to make you feel
just how much you mean to me,
how every thought, every heartbeat,
somehow leads me back to you.

But maybe there's no way for you to know,
no way for you to see
the depth of what I have carried
all this time.

I spent so long believing
that you didn't love me,
but now I wonder—
maybe you did,
maybe you do.

Maybe you were too scared to say it,
too lost to show it,
too tired to fight for it.

Or maybe you gave up.
Maybe you are still holding on.
Maybe not.
And maybe I will never know.

I am not sure what else I should cling to,
so I hold on to the only thing that's real—
the love I feel for you.
Because whether or not you ever reach back,
whether or not you ever say my name
with the same ache in your voice,
it doesn't change what's inside me.

I no longer wait for answers,
for confessions,
for clarity.
Maybe I will never figure out
what you truly wanted,
what you truly felt,
but I know one thing—
I will be here,
always,
waiting for that one moment

when fate allows me to be yours.

Maybe I deserve that happiness.
Maybe I don't.
But I know this—
I am not ready to give up.
Not on you.
Not on us.

Love you, always & forever.

Almost Together, Always Apart

We have never met,
never traced the lines of each other's hands,
never felt the warmth of an embrace
that lingers long after letting go.
Yet still, I have lived every moment with you,
felt every whisper slip between the silence,
as if love needed no touch to be real.

The screen stood between us,
a fragile wall,
a cruel reminder
that love can be close, yet still so far.
That no matter how many words we spill,
no matter how much laughter fills the space between,
I could never reach beyond the glass,
never pull you into my arms
and call you home.

Reality struck like a storm,

a bitter truth I could never escape—
that you were there, just beyond reach,
and I could never trace your heartbeat
beneath my trembling fingers.
I longed to press my ear to your chest,
to hear the steady rhythm of your existence,
to know for certain that you are real,
not just a dream I wake from too soon.

I craved the feel of your breath against mine,
the way your arms might fold into my body,
fitting like a missing piece
I have searched for my entire life.
I longed to hold you, just once,
just long enough
for time to forget we were ever apart.

Even now, the memories linger—
so fresh, so vivid,
as if just this morning,
I kissed your forehead,
watched your sleepy eyes meet mine,
whispered a quiet "good morning"
before the world awoke.
As if I had reached across the distance,
broken through the barriers,
and lived in a love that was never meant to be confined.

Damn—
I felt it as real as life itself.
As real as the ache that follows.
As real as the love that remains.

In the Silence, You Remain

Each day, I meet your presence anew,
In the echoes of a love once true.
Your reflection fades from my mirror's sight,
Yet lingers still in the hush of night.

I gather myself in scattered sheets,
Where once you lay in my embrace.
Your scent, woven into my pillow,
Rushes through me like liquid fire.

The rhythm of your racing heart
Still hums within these empty walls.
My ears have counted every breath,
Each whisper time refuses to steal.

The moonlight melts in your longing eyes,
While silent stars crumble in prayer.
Our betrayals lie between the nights,
Secrets carved in sleepless air.

I trace your name on fogged-up glass,
The letters fading as I sigh.
Each whispered syllable still clings,
To the spaces where your laughter died.

The wind still hums your favorite song,
A melody woven in the past.
But no voice answers when I call,
No hand to hold, no heart to last.

Each morning, I chase your shadow,
Hoping fate might make us collide.
Yet when I return, weary and lost,
I meet your presence once again.

No matter where my footsteps lead,
No matter how the seasons change,
You live in moments left behind,
In memories that never fade.

Your absence fills the spaces here,
More than your presence ever did.
And so, I roam this world alone,
A stranger in a life we lived.

Yet when the night unfolds its arms,
And silence hums a love once known,

I close my eyes and breathe you in,
For even in loss, you're still my home.

21

A Sinner for You

I gather the broken pieces of my heart,
scattered like fallen stars,
splintered by time, by distance, by love
that still lingers where it was left.

I do not mend them to move on,
not to forget,
not to heal—
but because you are still there,
tucked between the cracks,
resting in the ruins,
and I cannot keep you
in a place that is shattered.

So, I press the shards together,
even as they cut my hands,
even as they make me bleed.
Pain does not matter
when it is tied to you.
Every wound, every scar,

feels like a price worth paying
if it means keeping you here,
if it means you are not lost to me.

The world tells me to let go,
to turn away,
to cleanse myself of a love
that only echoes in the empty spaces.
But if loving you was a sin,
I would rather be a sinner,
again and again,
for lifetimes unending,
without repentance,
without regret.

For what is redemption
if it means losing you?
What is salvation
if it demands forgetting
the only thing
that ever made me feel alive?

So, do not worry if I break,
if my hands tremble as I try to rebuild
what love has left in ruins.
For I would rather walk this path,
wounded and weary,

than ever stand whole
in a world without you.

24

Born for the Darkness

My emotions are notorious when it comes to love,
Restless, reckless, untamed.
I was never the kind who could walk away
Without feeling the fire burn through my bones.
With me, everything was extreme—
When I loved, I drowned in it.
When I lost, I shattered.

She wasn't just love; she was my addiction.
A drug that ran wild in my veins,
A presence I needed like oxygen,
A voice that kept me alive in the silence.
I could not exist without her,
And when she left,
It felt like someone had gripped my throat
And demanded me to breathe.

I tried.
Oh, I tried.
But every gasp felt like fire,

Every breath was a battle I was losing.

So, I messed up—
Big time.
I drank until my bones felt like mist,
Until my body became numb,
Until my thoughts blurred into nothingness.
I smoked until I became the smoke,
Until I felt my insides burn
More than my heart already did.

I broke all the mirrors in my room,
Not because of anger,
But because I couldn't bear to see
The hollowed-out version of myself
Staring back at me.
I hated that reflection—
A stranger with my face,
A ghost of what I used to be.

So, I erased everything.
I threw away every memory,
Every trace of what once was.
I painted my walls black—
Dense, suffocating black.
Not because I loved the dark,
But because it was the only thing

That felt like home.

I wrapped myself in emptiness,
Welcomed the void like an old friend.
I let the silence whisper lullabies,
Kept every soul at a distance,
Built walls so high
That even I couldn't climb out.

So yes, maybe I'm not on the right track,
Maybe my destiny has slipped from my hands.
But maybe, just maybe,
I don't care anymore.
Maybe this is who I am now.
Maybe this is who I was always meant to be.

She once pulled me out of the darkness,
Made me believe in light,
But maybe I was never meant to stay there.
Maybe I was never meant to be saved.
Maybe the darkness was always calling me home.

And now, I am finally where I belong.

A Love Stuck in Pixels

How long must I exist in a world
where you are only a whisper,
a dream slipping through my fingers
before the morning steals you away?
I chase shadows of you in my sleep,
reaching for hands that never touch mine,
longing for lips that only exist in a memory
I've never truly lived.

I wish, just once,
that my imagination would surrender to reality,
that the universe would conspire
to turn my dreams into moments
I can finally call my own.
I don't want to spend forever
sending love through a lifeless screen,
trading warmth for words,
waiting for replies that never hold me back.

I'm tired of loving you through emojis,

of holding conversations that fill the void
but never the space beside me.
I don't want to describe how I feel—
I want you to see it,
feel it,
breathe it in the air between us.
I want to hold you close,
trace the outline of your soul
with my trembling fingers,
watch the fire in my heart
reflect in your eyes.

I don't want to type a goodnight,
watching three dots blink and disappear,
wondering if you're still there,
if you're thinking of me, too.
I want to pull you close,
lift you in my arms,
tuck you into bed where the world cannot reach us.

I want to kiss your forehead,
let my lips whisper a love
that words could never carry,
watch the moonlight melt into your gaze,
feel your breath sync with mine,
let silence speak
what distance has stolen.

I ache for a love that is tangible,
for moments where I no longer wake up
reaching for someone who isn't there.
I want to trade longing for presence,
imagination for reality,
dreams for nights where I no longer
have to wish for you—
because you'll already be here.

Love Was Never Meant for Me

Yes, it's not that I haven't been in love before.
I have felt it, breathed it, lived it.
I have built dreams upon whispered promises,
woven a future out of fragile hopes,
only to watch it all slip through my hands
like sand caught in the wind.

For ten years, I held onto love,
believed in forever, trusted in always.
And then, just like that,
forever turned into a memory,
always became never again.
The pain was relentless,
a storm that refused to pass,
a shadow that lingered
long after the sun had set.

I thought I'd never move on.
But I did.

Four years of drowning,
four years of searching
for a way to breathe without them,
four years of learning
how to exist with the weight
of love that no longer had a home.

And then, love found me again—
brief, fleeting, like a shooting star.
Three months of stolen moments,
three months of hope rekindled,
three months before it faded
into the same emptiness
that once swallowed me whole.

That's when I realized—
maybe love was never meant for me.

Every heartbreak carved its lesson
deep into my soul,
every goodbye left me changed
in ways I never expected.
I lost faith, lost belief,
lost the innocence
that once made love feel like magic.

Now, I stand at the edge of hope,
wondering if love is a dream
meant only for others,
if some hearts are built to break
but never to belong.

And maybe that's okay.
Maybe love is not a destination,
not a promise, not a guarantee.
Maybe love is just a passing storm,
a beautiful tragedy,
a lesson written in scars.

And maybe, just maybe,
I was never meant to stay in love—
only to survive it.

Epic, Even in Ruin

Like a million others, we too had a love story,
Born from whispers in a world of strangers,
Two voices lost in the hum of the unknown,
Two souls colliding across invisible miles.

It started as a passing moment,
A conversation on a random night,
A name glowing on my screen,
A voice that stirred something deep within.

At first, I laughed at the thought—
Love, stretching across unseen miles,
A connection formed not by touch, but by words,
Two hearts tethered by faith alone.

We spoke, we learned, we grew,
Strangers turned to something deeper,
Day by day, piece by piece,
We built a world only we could see.

Days were golden, nights were endless,
Drowning in the warmth of whispered confessions,
Tracing dreams into the silence,
Imagining the way our fingers would fit when entwined.

The nights were the hardest,
Lying awake, staring at a ceiling far from hers,
Wishing to reach through the screen,
To feel the softness of her breath against my skin.

I wished to hold her, to press her close,
To feel her laughter dance against my chest,
To know the weight of her presence beside me,
Not just the echo of her words.

But no matter how strong my longing burned,
She remained a heartbeat away—
So close, yet forever behind the glass of a screen,
A world we built, yet could never step into.

Everything was real—
The love, the passion, the aching devotion,
The dreams we stitched into the spaces between our
words,
The promises we made to a future we couldn't touch.

We whispered about the day distance would crumble,

The moment my arms would replace pixelated presence,
When my hands would cup her face instead of my own
longing,
When reality would match the love that already felt so
true.

But love is not just fire; it is also fragile,
A bridge of trust that sometimes trembles,
A story that bends under the weight of fate,
And no matter how we held on, the cracks began to
show.

Like all love stories that never find their forever,
Ours, too, met the dust of the unexpected,
Buried before we could make it bloom,
Yet even in its ruin, it was epic.

For love is not measured by how it ends,
But by the moments that made it eternal.

And even if we stand as strangers once more,
Even if silence has replaced our words,
I know—deep in the spaces where love still lingers—
That what we had was once everything.

And that will always be enough.

An Unfinished Forever

Yes, our story had a beautiful start,
woven with whispers, stitched with hearts.
Every word, every glance, every sigh,
felt like a promise under the endless sky.

I held your hand in the silence of night,
counting the stars, dreaming in light.
We spoke of tomorrows that seemed so sure,
of love unshaken, steady and pure.

I wished for a love that time wouldn't steal,
for a bond so strong, so pure, so real.
I dreamed of forever, hand in hand,
of a love that the world would understand.

But fate had threads of its own to weave,
pulling us apart with reasons unseen.
Not every love is meant to last,
some burn bright but fade too fast.

Still, I find you in the quiet of days,
in songs, in sunsets, in lingering ways.
You are the shadow my heart still knows,
the whisper in winds when the cold breeze blows.

I wonder if in some distant place,
we meet again in time and space.
Perhaps another world, another life,
where love's not bound by fate or strife.

Yet even though our tale remains untold,
left unwritten, left on hold,
it lingers in echoes, in memories deep,
an unfinished love, yet still so complete.

For some stories, though left undone,
are still the most epic ones.

Silent Goodbyes

We look into each other's eyes and smile,
Trying to pretend the pain is unforeseen,
Like strangers walking through a storm,
Convincing themselves the rain isn't real.

There was a phase—an awkward, aching pause,
Where we both knew what we feared to say,
That love, no matter how strong,
Sometimes bends beneath the weight of fate.

Yet, we still smiled.
Not because we were happy,
But because we were too afraid to cry.
Because if we did,
We knew the floodgates would open,
And we might never stop.

So we let our eyes do the talking,
Hoping they wouldn't betray the sorrow
That brewed beneath their surface.

Hoping they wouldn't reveal
The cracks forming beneath our skin,
The fractures in our hearts
That neither of us had the strength to mend.

We were breaking inside,
But neither of us dared to admit it.
Instead, we wrapped ourselves in silence,
Hoping a smile could hold us together.

We tried to be each other's strength,
Not by wiping away the tears,
But by making sure they never fell.
By swallowing the words
That could have shattered everything,
By choosing to hold on,
Even when our fingers were slipping.

We never fought to hurt each other,
We never screamed that it was over,
We never whispered that we should let go,
We never said that love had faded.

We never said anything at all.

Instead, we stood there,
Letting the silence speak,

Letting our unspoken words collide,
Scattering in different directions like shooting stars.

Maybe we believed that if we didn't say it,
It wouldn't be real.
Maybe we thought that silence
Could hold back the inevitable.

But love, even in silence,
Knows when it is being left behind.

And as we stood there, smiling through the pain,
We knew this was our silent goodbye.

Yet, even after we walked away,
Even after the distance settled between us,
I still see your face in my dreams.
I still hear your laughter in the echoes of my mind.
I still feel your presence in the quiet moments,
When the world is still,
And my heart aches for what once was.

I wonder if you do the same.
If you still think of me in the spaces between seconds,
If my name lingers on the tip of your tongue,
But never makes it past your lips.
If you ever wish you had turned back,

Even for just a second longer.

But love is cruel in the way it teaches us,
And sometimes the hardest lesson
Is learning to live with what was left unsaid.

So, I'll keep walking forward,
Carrying the weight of our silence,
Knowing that somewhere,
In another time, another life,
Perhaps we'll find the words we never said,
And we won't have to say goodbye.

If I Had Never Met You

It would have been different,
If I had never met you.
No need to chase your shadow,
No need to paint my world in the colors of your
presence,
No need to hold onto dreams that never woke up with
us.

No need to crave your touch in an empty room,
No need to search for you in the echoes of my heartbeat,
No need to love you in silence,
Hoping that maybe, just maybe,
You'd hear the whispers of my soul.

No need for heartbreaks that carve my ribs,
For tears that taste like your absence,
For words swallowed in the hollowness of goodbyes
unspoken.

No need for the way your name burns my lips,

The way your memories wrap around me like vines,
Pulling me deeper into a past that refuses to die.

No need for rejected hugs,
For kisses that never reached your lips,
For the ache of wanting
What was never mine to hold.

No need for sleepless nights spent talking to the moon,
Hoping it would carry my words to you,
No need for drowning in memories that refuse to let go,
For pretending you cared
When you only loved the way I made you feel.

No need for the moments
Where I stood before you, exposed,
Heart in my hands, trembling,
Only to watch you turn away.

No need for the slow unraveling,
For the silent war between my mind and my heart,
For the way I screamed into my pillow,
Wishing the pain would stop echoing back.

No need for the way you made me feel
Like absolutely nothing.

But I met you,
And now I live with the aftermath of loving a ghost.
A love that was real in my heart,
But never in yours.

How do you know it's over?
Maybe when you feel more in love
With the memories
Than with the person standing in front of you.

Maybe when the echoes of laughter
Feel louder than the silence you left behind.
Maybe when the ache becomes a lullaby,
A familiar song of longing and loss.

I tell myself I'm healing,
But some wounds never close—
They just become a part of who you are.

They become the poetry in my veins,
The ink in my sorrow,
The reason I still dream of you,
Even when I no longer want to.

The Silence of the Storm

There is a war inside me,
a battle of voices—pulling, tearing, demanding—
yet outside, the world only sees
a man standing still.

I want to scream—
not for attention, not for help,
but to release the weight
of everything I cannot say.
But if I scream, someone might hear.
And if they hear, they might see me break.
And if they see me break, they might know—
I am not as strong as I pretend to be.

So, I hold it in.
I choke on my own cries,
swallow my own suffering,
lock my pain behind a steady gaze.
Because in this world, strength is not a feeling—
it is a performance.

And I cannot afford to fall out of character.

But God, I am tired.
Tired of pretending I know where I'm going
when every step feels like sinking.
Tired of wearing strength like armor
when all it does is weigh me down.
Tired of feeling everything so deeply,
yet having nowhere to place it,
no hands to hold it,
no space safe enough to simply say—
I am not okay.

And maybe that is the worst part.
Not the pain. Not the confusion.
But the silence.
The unbearable, deafening silence
of a storm that has nowhere to break.

Screams in the Pillow

Every night, I crush my face into the pillow,
as if burying my pain could make it disappear.
I scream—loud enough to shatter the silence,
but not loud enough for the world to hear.

The walls stand still, indifferent and cold,
unshaken by the storms within my chest.
The moon watches with quiet pity,
but offers no solace, no place to rest.

I let out the cries I swallowed all day,
the words I wish I had the strength to say.
Pain twists in me like a clenched fist,
but no one knows—I hide it away.

The weight of everything I cannot control,
everything I have lost,
everything I will never be,
presses against my ribs,
crushing me from the inside out.

My screams do not beg for help,
they do not ask for comfort or saving.
They are not for anyone but me—
a desperate release, a breaking,
a way to feel something
other than this silent ache.

I scream for the moments I was unheard,
for the nights I felt invisible,
for the love that left me hollow,
for the battles I fight alone.

The pillow muffles my agony,
but it does not take it away.
Tears soak into the fabric,
but no one will ever see them.
By morning, the evidence is gone,
but the pain remains, a loyal shadow.

And so I rise with tired eyes,
carrying the weight of unspoken sorrow.
Pretending, performing, surviving—
until night falls again,
and the pillow swallows my screams once more.

Let Me Be, Just This Once

When I say I want to be left alone,
It's not because I don't care about the ones who claim to
stand by me,
Not because I don't see their concern in their eyes,
But because I am drowning in a storm
That even I cannot navigate.

There are days when my own reflection
Feels like a stranger staring back at me,
When my thoughts weave into endless loops,
Entangled in questions with no answers.
They ask me to explain,
To put into words what even my soul cannot decipher.
They wait, expecting something—
A confession, a reason, a neatly wrapped explanation.
But how do you explain a hurricane to those
Who have only ever known the breeze?

They come with their comforting words,
Handing them out like bandages for wounds they cannot

see:
"Forget."
"Smile."
"Leave it behind."
"Everything will be fine."
"You think too much."

But how do I forget
What has burned itself into my skin?
How do I smile
When my heart feels like it's held together by stitches
made of sorrow?
How do I leave it behind
When it has built a home within me,
Occupying every empty space I have left?

They won't let me be,
Won't let me sit in silence,
Won't let me grieve in peace.
Instead, they hover, waiting for a reaction,
For an outburst, for proof that I am breaking—
Not because they care,
But because they need to feel like they tried.

And when the weight of it all presses too hard against
my ribs,
When my voice cracks beneath the pressure,

When I let out even a fraction of the storm inside me,
The world shifts.
Suddenly, I am no longer the broken one,
No longer the one gasping for air.

Instead, I become the villain.

Arrogant.
Frustrated.
Irritating.
Selfish.
Disrespectful.

And just like that,
The narrative changes.
They are the victims now,
And I?
I am just the hurricane that came crashing into their
perfect sky.

But tell me—
Is it truly a crime to seek solitude
When my own thoughts are loud enough to deafen me?
Is it wrong to carve out space for my aching heart
When the world outside feels heavier than the one I
carry within?

If only they knew—
Sometimes, silence is not an escape,
It's survival.

If only they understood—
Some storms are not meant to be calmed,
Some hearts are not seeking to be fixed,
And some souls,
No matter how lost,
Just need to be left alone.

Drowning in a Crowd

I walk through the world with a borrowed smile,
a mask sculpted from expectations and duty.
They see what I allow, nothing more, nothing less—
a version of me that fits neatly into their world.
But beneath the surface, beneath the rehearsed facade,
my mind is a battlefield, my soul a ghost town.

Crowded trains swallow me whole,
surrounded by strangers, yet utterly alone.
Bodies brush past, voices rise and fall,
but their warmth never reaches me.
I am an island in a sea of movement,
adrift in thoughts too heavy to carry,
yet too ingrained to set down.

I lose myself in the blur of passing faces,
forget the stations, forget the stops.
The world outside races forward,
but I remain still, trapped in my own echoes.
The sun glares above, golden and warm,

but inside, I am nothing but winter—
frozen in a darkness I cannot escape.

A million times, I claw my way back,
force myself into conversations, into laughter.
A billion times, I slip away again,
pulled under by the tide of my own silence.

By night, the loneliness thickens,
a presence that wraps itself around me.
It knows my name, it whispers my fears,
reminding me of every scar I pretend not to see.
I become weightless in its grip,
drifting between memory and misery,
between what was and what could never be.

The walls know my secrets, the pillow holds my screams.
I press my face against the fabric,
muffling the sound of a breaking heart,
of pain that has no words, no release,
only an endless, suffocating presence.

Tears fall like unspoken confessions,
wet trails mapping the history of my suffering.
I cry and cry until my body betrays me,
until exhaustion forces my mind to surrender.
Sleep is not rest, only a temporary escape,

a moment where the ache fades into the void—
until morning calls me back to the cycle.

And so, I wake, as I always do,
putting on the same weary smile,
walking the same roads, saying the same words,
while no one notices how many times I have been lost,
or how many times I will lose myself again.

A Stranger in My Own Skin

My emotions lie scattered,
like shattered glass across the floor.
Somewhere in the wreckage,
the person I once was
has faded into someone I no longer recognize.

I have worn too many masks,
spoken in voices that weren't mine,
shaped myself into versions
that made others comfortable,
that made me acceptable.

Because the bitter truth of this world is—
people do not embrace you as you are.
They search for fragments they admire,
and only then do you become worthy
of their care,
their attention,
their love.

Nobody truly wants your story.
They listen,
but not to hear—
only to respond.
Only to fill the silence
with advice you never asked for,
with words that weigh more
than the pain you already carry.

Sometimes, we don't need solutions.
Sometimes, we don't need lessons.
Sometimes, all we need
is someone to just listen,
without judgment,
without corrections,
without telling us
how wrong we were,
or how broken we've become.

But silence is a rare gift.
And understanding, even rarer.
So here I stand,
tangled between who I am
and who the world expects me to be,
wondering if I will ever be enough
just as I am.

Love is a Lie

I sit in silence, staring at nothing,
Wondering how it all came to this.
I gave her my time, my love, my trust,
But none of it mattered—none of it.

She never cared, never saw me,
Took my heart like a passing thought.
Used it, drained it, left it empty,
Like it was something cheaply bought.

I thought love was real, unshaken,
A force that two hearts could hold.
But she proved me wrong with her absence,
Turned warmth into something cold.

Now love is just a word to me,
A lie we tell to ease the ache.
A fleeting spark, a fading dream,
A promise made just to break.

I'm done with love—I won't do it again,
Won't let someone pull me near,
Just to leave when they grow tired,
And make my heart disappear.

They say that time will heal the wounds,
That one day, I'll love again.
But how do you trust when you've been burned?
How do you risk the same pain?

So I build my walls, make them stronger,
Keep the world locked out for good.
No one can hurt what they can't reach,
No one will, even if they could.

I watch the days pass, feeling nothing,
A ghost in my own skin.
What is love but a cruel illusion?
A game that no one wins.

I don't believe in love anymore,
And I don't think I ever will.
It's safer here, in the quiet,
Where my heart stays safe and still.

Between Love and

Loneliness

She Was My Life, Now She's Gone

That evening still lingers, heavy in my chest,
The last time she held my hand, the final caress.
Her fingers trembled, her breath was light,
Like she had something to say, but chose the night.

Her eyes, a storm—restless, deep,
A silent scream, a wound that weeps.
I searched her face, hoping, praying,
That what I feared was not what she was saying.

But silence spoke in bitter tones,
And in that hush, I stood alone.
She let go, and in that space,
She left a void I still can't replace.

She walked away without a word,
Yet left behind echoes I still have heard.

A shadow imprinted deep in my soul,
A love that was whole, now just a hole.

A House Without Her

The walls still whisper where her laughter once danced,
The air still holds her ghost in a trance.
The scent of her lingers in places she stood,
Like the wind still remembers where she once would.

The sun still rises, the world still turns,
Yet without her, nothing truly burns.
The coffee brews, the clock still chimes,
But in this house, it's just borrowed time.

The morning light lacks its golden hue,
The nights stretch longer, cold and blue.
This house, this space, once warm, now bare,
Every corner screaming that she's not there.

Her footprints have faded, yet I still see,
The ghost of her walking right next to me.
Her absence lingers, it fills the air,
Yet when I reach for her, there's nothing there.

The Weight of Memory

I wake up each day, lost in the past,
Reliving a love that didn't last.
Her voice, her touch, her sweetest lies,
Play in my head, though she's nowhere in sight.

People say, *"Time will heal."*
But what do they know of the love I feel?
Wounds fade, but this one stays,
A hollow ache that never decays.

I reach for her in empty air,
A fool who hopes when no one's there.
If she returned, would it all be the same?
Or was I just a piece in her fleeting game?

I speak her name, but no one replies,
Only the wind sings lullabies.
She loved, she left, and now I stand,
Holding pieces of her in my trembling hands.

Does She Remember?

Some nights I wonder, does she think of me?
Or am I just dust in her history?
A moment she lived, a name she forgot,
While I stay here, lost in thought.

Does she ever pause in the middle of her day,
Hear a song, taste the air, feel the weight?
Do memories flood, do they make her sigh?
Or was I nothing—just a passerby?

I wonder if her heart ever aches the same,
If my name still lingers like an unshaken flame.
Or am I the love she buried deep,
A story untold, a secret to keep?

The Man I've Become

I am undone, I am torn,
A man who loved, a heart still worn.
Maybe this pain will never end,
For she was my life—
And now, I am just pretend.

I don't know how to unlove, how to forget,
How to move on with a heart filled with regret.
The walls around me, I built them high,
To keep her out, to lock me inside.

Love is a lie, a cruel disguise,
A promise that fades before your eyes.
I won't be fooled, I won't believe,
For love is just a game that leaves.

And so I sit, night after night,
Drenched in memories, losing the fight.
Maybe one day, this weight will fade,
But until then, I live in the shade.

For she was my life, my light, my home,
And now, I walk this world alone.

If You Hold Me Too Long

If you hold me too long, you may glimpse the hidden
truth
beneath the smile you've always known—
the person you think is unbreakable,
the one who stands strong against every storm,
is a delicate soul quietly unraveling in your arms.

I wear my strength like a carefully chosen mask,
a smile that lights up the world on the surface,
but inside, there's a soft, trembling heart
burdened by whispers of sorrow and unspoken fears.
Every embrace peels away a layer of pretense,
revealing a raw, unguarded vulnerability
that I've spent a lifetime concealing.

In your gentle hold, you'll feel the subtle quake
of a spirit overwhelmed by the weight of its own
fragility—
a soul that has learned to shield itself behind laughter
while quietly mourning the battles fought alone.

I am a mosaic of tender fragments:
shards of long-forgotten dreams,
traces of tears that have never dried,
each piece a silent testament to the pain I hide.

I have carried storms within me,
tucked them beneath my ribs,
hid them behind a well-rehearsed grin
so no one would ever see the weight of them.
But if you hold me for too long,
you might feel the thunder rumbling inside my chest,
the way my breath catches in a moment of surrender,
the way my body tenses before it dares to fall apart.

I am tired of being the strong one,
the one who listens, the one who carries,
the one who holds everything together
while quietly crumbling behind closed doors.
I have spent years convincing the world
that I do not need saving,
but the truth is—
I have longed for someone to notice the cracks,
to run their fingers gently over the fractures
and not turn away from the damage they find.

Every second of closeness is a double-edged gift,
offering comfort even as it unmasks the truth:

I am not the perpetual beacon of joy you admire,
but a human being who aches with quiet desperation,
yearning for understanding, for solace that speaks
to the broken parts of me.
In that extended, heartfelt embrace, you might sense
the deep, unyielding loneliness behind my eyes,
a profound vulnerability that I never wished to reveal.

And maybe, just maybe, you will understand
that my silence has never meant I was okay,
that my strength has never been effortless,
that the weight of my own mind is heavier
than I have ever let on.
Perhaps in that moment,
with your arms wrapped around me,
you will feel the unspoken exhaustion of a heart
that has been strong for far too long.

So if you hold me for too long,
please do so with tenderness and care—
for in that unguarded moment, you meet not just
the strong, smiling face of the person you've always
known,
but the fragile, wounded soul beneath,
whispering its silent plea for healing
in the quiet, unspoken language of true intimacy.

The Me You Erased

For years, you shaped me, molded me,
turned me into the version you wanted to see.
Piece by piece, I let go of myself,
adapting, shifting, bending to fit
the image you painted of me.

I forgot the sound of my own voice,
buried my dreams beneath your expectations,
lost sight of the person I used to be—
all for the sake of keeping you close,
all for the hope that I'd be enough.

I let your words guide me like a sculptor's hands,
chipping away at the parts of me that didn't fit,
smoothing the rough edges of my thoughts,
reshaping my laughter, quieting my protests.
And I let you, because I thought love meant sacrifice,
because I thought if I became what you wanted,
maybe then, I'd finally be worthy of staying.

But now, you stand before me,
searching for someone I no longer recognize,
asking for the one you once knew,
the soul I left behind in the process of becoming yours.
And I try, I try so hard to remember—
but when I reach inside myself,
I find nothing but echoes of a self long erased.

Tell me, how do I return to a version of me
that no longer exists?
How do I gather the shattered fragments
of a person I barely remember?
You made me into this, reshaped my edges,
and now you beg for what you destroyed.

I spent years contorting myself to fit into your world,
only to wake up one day
and find that I no longer belonged in my own.
I look in the mirror,
but the reflection is unfamiliar,
a stranger wearing my skin,
a hollow frame filled with expectations that were never
mine.

Now, you want me to go back,
to return to the soul I once carried so freely,
but tell me—

how can I retrace my steps
when every road leads back to you?
How do I breathe life back into a fire
that you spent years extinguishing?

I am lost between who I was and who you made me.
And maybe, just maybe, it's time
I start becoming who I was meant to be—
without you.

The Cost of Being Loved

Why can't anyone ever accept us as we are?
Why must we always be reshaped,
trimmed down, painted over,
turned into something easier to love,
easier to understand,
easier to fit into their perfect little worlds?

Everybody is always looking,
searching for a version of us
that pleases their eyes,
that satisfies their expectations,
that makes them feel comfortable in our presence.
It doesn't matter if that version
is a mask we wear with trembling hands,
a lie whispered so often
it begins to feel like the truth.

They say they love us,
but only when we shrink ourselves down
to fit into the space they have reserved for us.

They admire us,
but only when we shine in ways
that reflect their own desires.
They care,
but only for the parts that make them feel whole,
never for the pieces of us
that are messy, complicated, untamed.

And so, we bend.
We soften our edges,
dim our brilliance,
suppress the wild, aching parts of our souls
that refuse to be tamed.
We trade authenticity for acceptance,
silence our truth in exchange for belonging.

But what happens when the weight of it all
becomes too heavy to carry?
What happens when we look in the mirror
and no longer recognize the reflection staring back?
What happens when we realize
we have spent so long becoming
who they wanted us to be
that we no longer remember who we were?

It doesn't even matter, they say,
if you lose yourself

in the process of making them happy.
But it should.
It should matter more than anything.
Because what is love,
what is acceptance,
if it comes at the cost of our own existence?

One day, I will stop apologizing
for the space I take up,
for the way my heart beats,
for the way my soul refuses to fit
into a shape that is not its own.
One day, I will be enough
just as I am—
not for them,
but for me.

Love Shouldn't Hurt

Meeting you will never be my regret,
but tolerating the ways you hurt me, always will be.
I will never wish away the moment our eyes first met,
the way your laughter felt like music,
or the way my heart learned to beat
to the rhythm of your presence.

You were a chapter I never wanted to skip,
a story I once believed in,
a home I tried to build with bare hands,
even as the walls crumbled around me.
I let love blind me to the cracks,
convinced myself that pain was just
the price of something real,
that love could fix what was breaking me.

I made excuses when you left me waiting,
rewrote your indifference as a temporary storm,
one I believed you would calm with time.
I convinced myself that if I just held on longer,

if I just loved a little harder,
you would finally see me,
finally cherish me
the way I so desperately wished you would.

But love should never feel like begging.
Love should never feel like enduring.
And yet, I sat there,
tolerating every wound disguised as an accident,
every word that cut but never healed,
every moment you made me feel like I was
too much and never enough all at once.

I swallowed my pain,
buried it beneath whispered reassurances—
"It will get better."
"They didn't mean it."
"This is just how love is."
But love is not supposed to leave you hollow.
Love is not supposed to feel like a war
where you are the only one fighting.

So I let you go,
not because I stopped caring,
but because I started caring for myself.
I will never regret the way I loved you,
but I will always regret

the way I let myself suffer for you.

Meeting you will never be my regret,
but the way I let your love consume me—
that, I will never forgive myself for.

The First and The Last

You were the first person I ever showed my heart to,
the first to see the pieces I kept hidden,
the first to touch the scars I never spoke of,
the first to hold the weight of my quietest fears.
I gave you every unspoken truth,
every fragile hope I had buried deep,
every part of me I had always been afraid to share—
and you held it in your hands like it meant nothing at all.

I let down my walls for you,
let you walk through doors I never opened for anyone
else.
I let you see me—not the version of me the world
expected,
not the smile I wore like armor,
but the real, raw, unguarded soul beneath.
And for a moment, I thought that was enough.
I thought I was enough.

But love in your hands was never gentle.

It was careless, sharp-edged, and heavy,
filled with promises that felt real
until they turned to dust in my grasp.
You saw my heart,
held it for just long enough to make me believe,
then let it slip through your fingers
like it was never worth holding onto at all.

You were the first person I ever trusted,
and the last I ever will.
Because now, I know better.
Now, I know that love is not always a sanctuary,
that not every embrace means safety,
that sometimes, the ones who hold you close
are the same ones who will tear you apart.

I remember the way I used to look at you,
like you were the safest place in the world.
How foolish I was to believe
that love could not also be destruction,
that the hands meant to hold me
would be the same ones to let me fall.
I learned that day what heartbreak really is—
not loud, not violent, but silent and slow,
like the fading warmth of a fire left to die.

I tried to understand, tried to rationalize,

tried to make sense of the way you loved me
only when it was convenient,
only when it didn't require effort,
only when I was easy to love.
I convinced myself that if I just gave more,
if I just held on longer,
maybe you would finally see my worth.
But love is not something to be earned,
and I should have never had to beg for it.

You made me believe I was safe,
only to turn love into something terrifying.
I started to fear the very thing I once longed for,
pulling away from hands that reached out to me,
because I knew how it felt
to be held only to be dropped.

I no longer wear my heart on my sleeve,
no longer let anyone close enough
to feel its quiet ache, its steady beat.
I have locked it away, sealed behind walls
that no one will ever climb again.
Not because I don't want to be loved,
but because I won't risk being destroyed.

Now, when love knocks, I do not answer.
Now, when someone asks me to trust them,

I only smile,
because I know how quickly love can turn cold.
I know how promises can be made
with the same lips that will one day say goodbye.
I know that some people only love
until it no longer suits them.

You were the first person I ever showed my heart to,
and you are the reason no one will ever see it again.

Walking Away

I wanted to feel loved
without feeling like I had to beg for it,
without stretching my hands out
only to grasp at empty air,
without whispering my worth
to someone who never truly listened.

Love should not feel like a desperate plea,
like knocking on a door that never opens,
like waiting for rain in a desert
that has long since forgotten the taste of water.
I stood there for so long,
hoping, believing, convincing myself
that if I just gave a little more,
held on a little tighter,
you would see me,
you would choose me.

But love should never be a performance,
a never-ending audition

for a role I was never meant to play.
It should not be something I have to earn,
something I have to prove,
something I have to fight for
when my heart is already exhausted.
Love should be given, freely,
without hesitation, without conditions,
without the need to constantly remind you
that I am here,
that I exist,
that I deserve to be cherished.

I spent too many nights
waiting for words that never came,
for gestures that always fell short,
for proof that I mattered to you
the way you mattered to me.
But love should not leave me questioning,
should not make me feel invisible,
should not make me wonder
if I am asking for too much
when all I ever wanted
was to feel wanted.

So I gave up.
Not because I stopped loving you,
but because I started loving myself more.

Because I could no longer stand
to feel like a stranger in my own heart,
to watch myself disappear
in the pursuit of something
that should have never needed chasing.

I gave up because love
should never feel like a battle
where only one of us is fighting.
And I am done fighting
for a love that never fought for me.

When I Am Just a Memory

Someday, when my name is nothing but a whisper—
fading like the last notes of a song no one remembers,
a breath lost to the wind, a story left unfinished,
perhaps then, in the silence I leave behind,
you will finally understand what it meant to be unseen.

I stood before you, my soul stripped bare,
hands trembling as I held out my heart—
a fragile offering you never cared to take.
I spoke in the language of longing,
in sighs too soft, in wounds too deep,
in the aching quiet between your laughter.
But you never listened.

I was there, in the pauses you never noticed,
in the spaces your love never reached,
in the shadow cast by your sun,
waiting for you to turn and see me.
Waiting for the impossible.

You loved the world with wild abandon,
chased everything but me,
spilled your heart into hands that never stayed,
while I stood still, unseen, unheard,
a whisper against the roar of all you wanted.

Did you ever see the way my fingers trembled
when I reached for something you never gave?
Did you hear the quiet war inside me—
the silent screams of wanting to be enough,
the relentless battle between hope and surrender?

One day—one inevitable, cruel day—
when my absence wraps around you
like the weight of everything you never said,
perhaps then, and only then,
you will search for me
in the echoes of places I no longer exist.

Maybe you'll hear my laughter in the wind,
see a glimpse of me in the eyes of a stranger,
wake up reaching for a warmth long gone,
only to find your hands clutching nothing but ghosts.

And when you whisper my name in the dark,
realizing it no longer belongs to your lips,
when you taste regret like rust on your tongue,

perhaps then—just for a fleeting, agonizing second—
you will know what it was like to be me.

But by then, I will be nothing more than dust,
drifting through the cracks of time,
a name too faint to hold,
a love you forgot to cherish
while it was still alive.